THE PATH OF THE SEER

First Edition.

All content enquiries to cleland@freedomhouse.biz

First published 2020.

Cover image—Copyright: franckreporter

THE PATH OF THE SEER

BY THE SAME AUTHOR

MOSES, THE MAKING OF A LEADER. Published by Kingsway in the UK and Victory Press in America. Book of the day at Spring Harvest.

ABRAHAM, FRIEND OF GOD. Published by Kingsway.

BROKEN HEARTED BELIEVERS. Published by Kingsway in the UK and Karas Sana in Finland.

FRIENDS OF GOD. Co-written with Jeff Lucas. Published by Crossway.

THE POWER TO PERSUADE. Published by Pioneer.

DESTINY CALLS, first edition. Published by Canaan Press. Ghost-written for Norman and Grace Barnes.

QUESTIONABLE SUPERNATURAL. Published by Amazon.

DESTINY CALLS, second edition. Published by Clean Copy Editing. Ghost-written for Norman and Grace Barnes.

DEDICATION

I'd like to dedicate this book to the amazing group of people who pray and laugh alongside me. They are affectionately known as the Banana Bunch, and living proof that ... 'Whoever believes in me will do the works I have been doing, and they will do even greater things than these.'

DONATIONS

I do not make any money from my books, podcasts, or resources.

Any cost of this book covers Amazon's fees. All other income goes to the charity.

CONTENTS

CHAPTER 1

Getting Started

Baby steps

You don't have to teach a baby to see. If its sight isn't impaired, it will simply open its eyes and look around.

Babies eventually need help to *understand* what they see. But seeing is as natural as breathing.

It's the same with spiritual sight. However, God must open your eyes first.

In 2 Kings 6, Elisha's servant was afraid because he was surrounded by the enemy's armies. So, Elisha prayed (v17): 'Open his eyes Lord, so that he may see.' When the servant looked again, he saw horses and chariots of fire.

Only God can give spiritual sight. We cannot 'activate' it and we shouldn't try to.

I started 'seeing' spiritual things soon after I became a Christian.

I did not ask for this ability and cannot claim any credit for it. I did not earn it, and sometimes ask God to take it away. It can be hard to cope with the things he shows you, and people rarely accept your insights.

I first used it to help a close friend. God showed me that he was struggling with emotional problems. He cried when I told him what I had seen. So, we prayed, and God miraculously freed him.

A similar thing happened a few weeks later. I impulsively drove to another friend's house at 1am to tell him what God had shown me.

He wasn't too grateful for being dragged out of bed. But he was very appreciative when Jesus freed him from a problem which went back to his childhood.

I was more surprised than he was. I was a very new Christian, and I couldn't make sense of it all.

Forty-five years later, I still can't.

A life-changing Bible study

Around the same time, I had a dramatic encounter with God.

I was sitting in my lounge, reading Luke 1, and as I turned the page to verse 76, his power hit me. I found myself faced down on the floor.

The room was filled with a shocking sense of the Father's love and majesty.

I didn't know how to respond, so I sat up and breathlessly picked up my Bible.

God literally burned the words from verse 76 into my spirit: 'And you, my child, will be called a prophet of the Most High, for you will go on before the Lord to prepare the way for him, to give his people the knowledge of salvation through the forgiveness of their sins.'

I gasped: 'Lord, how on earth can that happen?'

God hadn't finished. There was a knock on the door.

I opened it, but there was no one there. The street was deserted. Then, I noticed a small card lying on the doormat. It had Psalm 37:5 written on it: 'Commit your way to the Lord; trust in Him, and He will do it.'

The power of God enveloped me again, and I fell to the floor. I was never the same again.

I had begun an extraordinary journey of joy, miracles, pain, and tears.

I never call myself a prophet. Luke 1:76 says: 'You will be *called* a prophet,' so it's for others to decide what I am.

Prophets in the Bible rarely gave themselves a title. They did not need to. In fact, Amos said he wasn't one.

I get nervous when Christians give themselves titles. Being a Reverend doesn't make you reverent and calling yourself a leader doesn't mean that people will follow you.

Christian service is about who we are, not what we call ourselves. This is why Paul said in 2 Corinthians 10:12: 'We do not dare to classify ourselves.'

So, since that shocking afternoon in 1978, I have offered God my senses, and he does the rest, despite my many flaws, fears, and insecurities.

I've had some great companions along the way.

One of them is Norman Page, another seer. He is one of the wisest men I've met and has contributed to this book.

What is a seer?

The Old Testament mentions prophets and seers. They are different.

Prophets hear and say. But seers see and pray.

So, prophets pass on the Lord's messages. God explains in Deuteronomy 18:18: 'I will raise up a prophet ... and I will put my words in his mouth, and he shall speak ...'

Seers are different. Some receive visions and pictures from God concerning the past, present and future. Others can see people's characters, sins, motives, and gifts.

Some have heavenly encounters and see things in the spiritual realm. They understand what God is doing in different situations and can interpret supernatural activity.

There are several examples in the Old Testament. 2 Chronicles 29: 25 mentions Gad the king's seer. Gad is also mentioned in 2 Samuel 24:11.

Samuel was better known as a prophet but is also described as a seer in 1 Chronicles 29:29.

And 1 Samuel 9:9 describes how the roles of prophet and seer developed: 'Formerly in Israel, if someone went to inquire of God, they would say: "Come, let us go to the seer," because the prophet of today used to be called a seer.'

There are two Hebrew words for a seer. One is *ra'ah,* which means to see visions; to perceive; to gaze, and to look upon.

The other word is *chozeh,* which is a beholder of a vision, or 'gazer'.

So, seers see, gaze, reflect, ponder, and pray. I started in primary school, where I was frequently told off for daydreaming!

Old Testament seers did not usually speak about what they saw unless they were asked to (see 1 Samuel 9:9).

Why? I believe it's because people only ask when they are hungry, or when they realise that they don't have answers. Then, they may be ready to hear.

One seer, called Hanai, tried speaking without being asked and ended up in prison (2 Chronicles 16: 7-10). Be warned. People don't always accept seers' revelations.

The roles of prophets and seers appear to have merged in the New Testament church. Ephesians 4:11 says: 'And he gave some apostles; and some *prophets;* and some evangelists; and some pastors and teachers.'

So, seers are now called prophets, although not all prophets are seers. Some people are both.

'Seeing' is not the same as the gift of discernment. Discernment is a gift of the Holy Spirit, whereas seers and prophets are empowered by God. Seers can usually discern spirits, and a lot more besides. But God sometimes uses the gift of discernment to introduce people to the spiritual realm.

Personally, I don't care what people call me. Some say I'm a seer; others say I'm a heretic, and they're probably both right.

However, 'seeing' is a strange gift, as I soon discovered …

The seer as an estate agent

A well-known evangelist once phoned and asked for my help. My ever-present ego inflated as I dreamt of speaking at Spring Harvest or accompanying him on a world tour.

But he merely asked: 'Can you help me sell my flat?' I was puzzled, as I had no experience in property dealing. It transpired that he needed prayer support.

He had been trying to sell his flat for two years, and the delay was frustrating God's plans. He was stuck.

I wasn't sure what I could do. But when I went around to pray, God showed me that an evil spirit was blocking the sale. So, we bound it and kicked it out of the building.

He sold the flat the following afternoon! He was overjoyed. I was shocked.

Then a similar thing happened a year later.

Another friend was a property developer and could not sell a flat that he had renovated.

It had been on the market for months, and he faced bankruptcy if he didn't sell it straight away.

We popped in there one lunchtime, and God showed me there was a curse on it. We broke it in Jesus' name, and the flat was sold two hours later.

It later transpired that my friend's former business partner had cursed the sale after a dispute. Words have power.

The Lord then gave me a break from 'property sales' until 2018. Then, a friend and his wife wanted to sell their flat and join a church in a village near me.

Twelve months later, they were still trying to sell it.

The Holy Spirit prompted me to pray by the village sign, where God showed me a 'gatekeeper' spirit who was keeping my friends out.

We bound it, and their move went ahead the same afternoon.

Prayer is not always enough

In each of these situations, prayer was not enough on its own. Each transaction needed spiritual insight and spiritual warfare as well.

Many Christians never engage in spiritual warfare or try to keep it 'respectable.'

They say that *praise* is warfare. It's not – it's praise. It can be used during warfare to encourage the troops and proclaim our victorious king. But it is not a substitute for warfare.

There is no biblical evidence that Satan's armies are vanquished through praise. They might retreat for a while, but they soon come back after the music stops.

Some people say that it was the musicians in Joshua's army who were responsible for the walls of Jericho crashing down.

But those mighty walls collapsed because of the Word of the Lord. Joshua 2: 1 says: 'Then the LORD said to Joshua: 'See, I have delivered Jericho into your hands, along with its king and its fighting men.'

Prayer is not warfare, either. When we pray, we speak to God. But when we wage spiritual warfare, we address the enemy. You will see limited results if you just do one.

In Ephesians, Paul taught about lifestyle, church unity, family life, and work. And then, having marked out the battle zones, he told us in Ephesians 6 to wrestle *with* spiritual forces of evil in the heavenly realms.

On another occasion, he also told us to wrestle *in* prayer, like Epaphras (Col 4:12).

You can see how it worked in Daniel 10:12. The young intercessor prayed, sought wisdom, and humbled himself, and God answered.

But Satan's angels delayed the Lord's response from reaching Daniel for 21 days. The Archangel Michael had to battle with the spiritual Princes of Greece and Persia to clear the way.

Nothing's changed.

But now, Jesus has now handed *us* the authority to join God's angels to fight those foul spiritual enemies who hinder God's purposes.

Sadly, most Christians never use it, and then get disillusioned when their prayers aren't answered.

Some don't even believe in the devil. Sadly, their unbelief just makes his job easier.

Time to fight?

It may be time for you to take up your sword and fight for your soul, your family, your church, and your workplace.

But if you join the battle, you will need God's 'sight' to see your enemies. Spiritual warfare is not a heavenly game of 'blind man's bluff'. This is why the Holy Spirit distributes the gift of discernment, and the book of Proverbs repeatedly encourages us to seek insight.

But 'seeing' is not a stunt and should never be misused. It is an aspect of God's love.

Paul said in Philippians 1:9-11: 'And this is my prayer: that your *love* may abound more and more in knowledge, and depth of *insight,* so that you may be able to *discern* what is best and may be pure and blameless for the day of Christ.'

Paul asked God to give the Ephesians wisdom and revelation and to open the eyes of their hearts.

I still pray that prayer most days. Try it. Your Christian life will become more effective, and you will see surprising results.

CHAPTER 2

What Seers See

The Bible is the only reliable guide for discovering what the Holy Spirit may show us.

Some people claim to have 'seen' everything from axes sticking out of people's heads to chains around their feet. But I cannot find any scriptural basis for revelations like these.

God may show us a picture that portrays someone's condition, or that reveals something about them. But it shouldn't be confused with the 'real thing.'

The spiritual realm is real. But we can end up in some bizarre places if we go beyond the scriptures.

These are the things that seers 'saw' in the Bible.

1. People's characters

In John 1:47 we discover: 'When Jesus *saw* Nathaniel approaching, he said of him: "Here truly is an Israelite in whom there is no deceit."'

Jesus wasn't referring to Nathaniel's behaviour or his reputation. The words '*in whom*' refer to what was *inside him*. Jesus had deep insight into Nathaniel's heart.

No one can truly know what's in someone else's heart unless God shows them.

Jeremiah 17:10 says: 'I the Lord search the heart and examine the mind to reward each person according to their conduct, according to what their deeds deserve.'

If we try to 'work people out' ourselves, we may become suspicious and create damaging theories. Human reasoning has little or no place in the life of the seer.

2. *The Holy Spirit's activity*

It's a wonderful privilege to see the Holy Spirit at work.

John the Baptist was a prophet and a seer, and he said (John 1:32): 'I *saw* the Spirit come down from heaven as a dove and remain on him.'

God may allow you to see the Spirit working in someone's life, or in a meeting, assuming, that is, he is given the chance amid the structures and liturgies!

It's exciting when you see him alight on someone, and then they start prophesying or speaking in tongues.

I once saw him descend on two girls, bearing the gifts of healing. I suggested that they pray for others, and when they did, people were healed.

It can be very frustrating, though, when you can see what the Holy Spirit wants to do, but the worship leader or person leading the meeting can't.

I believe churches would see far more spiritual power if leaders worked with seers.

3. *People's gifts*

I once noticed a church elder anointing someone with oil, and 'saw' he had a ministry in this area. I encouraged him and now he frequently anoints people in a unique way. God then heals and changes people.

The ability to 'see' people's gifts and ministries is entirely biblical.

In John 1:29, we read: 'The next day, John *saw* Jesus coming towards him, and said: "Look, the Lamb of God, who takes away the sin of the world."'

So, when John *saw* Jesus, he didn't just see his cousin, a 30-year-old Rabbi. He saw his calling.

The same happened to Jesus later in the chapter (v42). He *looked* at Peter and said: 'You are Simon, son of John. You will be called Cephas.'

He didn't just see a married man and a fisherman. One look revealed Peter's future ministry.

A similar thing happened in 2 Kings 2:15. 'Now when the sons of the prophets who were at Jericho *saw* him, they said: "The Spirit of Elijah does rest on Elisha."'

The sons of prophets *saw* God's anointing.

So, seers can play a significant part in identifying people's ministries and helping them find their roles in the body of Christ. They won't have all the answers, but they may provide useful insights.

It saddens me when churches use man-made aptitude tests to establish someone's gift. Seers may do a better job because God's calls and the Holy Spirit's gifts are discerned spiritually, not with an algorithm.

I was with one seer who addressed a church's leadership team. The church was struggling to grow.

He pointed to the pastor and said: 'You aren't the leader ... he is.' He pointed to another man.

This was difficult for the pastor. But he graciously stood down, and the church soon flourished.

However, this approach is risky.

I have known remote 'apostles' remove church leaders on a whim, or because they haven't met their performance targets. They ruined lives and even entire churches in the process.

This happens when apostles act without the input of seers.

Paul says in Ephesians 3: 20 that churches are built on the foundation of apostles *and* prophets, with Jesus as the cornerstone.

A prophet will usually be able to 'see' God's man. And, of course, any destructive apostolic decision is unlikely to have Jesus as the cornerstone.

4. *Angels and demons*

All kinds of people in the Bible saw angels.

Moses, Daniel, Gad, Ezekiel, and Joseph had visitations in the Old Testament and Mary, Joseph, Elizabeth, and some shepherds saw them in the New Testament.

They appeared to seers and non-seers alike. So, question anyone who suggests that they are special because they have had angelic visitations.

If God wants you to see an angel, you will. It's down to him, not you. And seeing an angel doesn't make you more significant than anyone else.

I am sceptical of people who say they have frequent encounters with angels. Strangely, many of them have TV shows or speak at conferences!

These experiences can produce 'super saints' who claim to walk in a higher revelation. They are a throwback to the Old Testament, where the Holy Spirit only rested on chosen individuals.

Paul warned about these 'super-apostles' in 2 Corinthians 11. No one in the body of Christ has a 'super' ministry. We're all made of dust. We're all clay pots that contain God's treasure. The day we think we otherwise may be the day God will start to withdraw his favour from us.

We should never seek angelic appearances. Angels take instructions from God, not us, and we cannot and should not summon them.

Hebrews 1:14 makes this clear: 'Are not all angels ministering spirits sent to serve those who will inherit salvation?'

Psalm 103:20 says that angels do God's bidding, not ours. Daniel 6:22 confirms this. When King Darius asked Daniel if he had survived a night in the lions' den, he replied: 'My God sent his angel, and he shut the mouths of the lions.'

Seers sometimes see Satan's angels and evil spirits, too. I have looked at this in greater detail in Chapter 9.

5. *People's sin.*

God sometimes shows seers and prophets people's sin.

Jesus did it with the woman at the well (John 4: 1-26). And the Lord used Nathan to expose King David's adultery and conspiracy to murder (2 Samuel 12: 1-15).

The Holt Spirit also revealed Ananias and Sapphira's lies and financial duplicity to Peter in considerable detail (Acts 5:1-11).

I find it difficult when I 'see' sin in other people's lives. I have enough problems dealing with my own stuff, let alone theirs!

And it's hard to know how to respond. What do you do when you can 'see' that a pastor is deceived, that a 'happily married' husband is having an affair, that a bridegroom clearly doesn't like his bride, that someone has a treacherous motive behind their impressive prayers, or that a husband is violently abusing his wife?

I recently 'saw' that a leading apostolic figure had seized another man's 'crown' and was ministering as a usurper. What did I do about it? Pray. Nothing else.

Exposing wrongdoing needs considerable discretion and great wisdom from the Holy Spirit. When it happens, God usually asks me to pray about it privately.

Seers require 'big' eyes and small mouths. They must file their observations, pray, and keep quiet until God creates an opportunity for them to share them.

Sometimes he doesn't, and you should never force it.

You can cause lasting damage if you share something too soon, or that is wrong, or that should remain concealed.

Concealed? Yes. Our first reaction should be to conceal someone's sin. That might surprise you in our 'whistle blower' culture. But 1 Peter 4: 8 says: 'Above all, love each other deeply, because love covers over a multitude of sins.'

The words *cover over* mean to conceal or to hide.

In addition, Proverbs 17:9 says: 'Whoever conceals an offense promotes love, but he who brings it up separates friends.'

Clearly, we need wisdom. There is a difference between *seeing* someone's sin and actually *knowing* about it.

Sometimes we have a moral and legal duty to inform a leader or the authorities about someone's behaviour. I usually only speak first if someone else is being harmed or at risk.

It can be difficult if the person denies what you have seen.

People may go to great lengths to hide their sins, and may recruit their friends, families, and leaders to prove you wrong.

In these cases, you must keep quiet, and let God have the final say.

Nathan 'went home' after confronting King David with his wrongdoing. That's the best approach. The seer's job is to pass on God's insights, not to get involved in the fallout.

Prophets and seers need to know when to go home. They may cause problems if they stay around a situation too long.

CHAPTER 3

The Slaughter of the Innocents

Destruction and grief

I learned early in my Christian life that seers have a vital role in spiritual warfare.

In Ephesians 6, Paul describes the importance of wearing the armour of God. He based his metaphors on the equipment used by Roman soldiers.

Their helmets covered their heads but left their eyes exposed. You can't fight your enemy if you can't see him.

And after describing the armour, Paul says in (v19): 'And pray in the spirit on all occasions with all kinds of prayers and requests.'

Seeing, praying, and fighting go together.

Soon after I became a Christian, I went to dinner with a young couple, and they shared a tragic story.

They had suffered a cot death the year before and were traumatised. Somehow, they had managed to persevere with their faith, despite deep torment and many unanswered questions.

We prayed, and they told me a horrifying story.

Several other couples in their small church had also suffered cot deaths during the previous few years, and another couple had lost an older daughter.

The church was in a state of shock and grief, and women feared getting pregnant.

I was so troubled, I went to a hilltop to pray and fast about it, and God showed me a vision of a sinister dark cloud over the church.

The church leaders did not believe in spiritual warfare, so I gathered a group to pray about it. It was my first venture into warfare in the heavenly places.

The Holy Spirit showed us that the cloud represented spirits of death over the church. We interceded and bound them, and the cot deaths stopped. But I was still unsure why such a tragic episode had occurred.

God showed me a few years later.

The deaths started after many members of the congregation visited a temple dedicated to other gods. They removed their shoes and took part in a wedding ceremony.

Now, I have no problem with other religions or their temples. God gives us the freedom to worship whoever and wherever we want.

But Christians must follow God's rules, the same as other faiths do.

Removing your shoes is a sign of worship, and the first commandment (Exodus 23:4-5) says: 'You shall not make for yourself an image in the form of anything in heaven above or on the earth beneath or in the waters below, bow down to them or worship them.

'For I, the Lord your God, am a jealous God, *punishing the children* for the sin of the parents to the third and fourth generation.'

It became tragically clear that this church paid a high price for compromising on God's word. Satan is out to kill.

If you worship other gods, you will be cursed. Many Christians struggle with this concept because they believe God will protect them.

But Psalm 91:10 says that his protection is conditional: 'If you say, "The LORD is my refuge," and you make the Most High your dwelling, no harm will overtake you, no disaster will come near your tent.'

God can only protect us *if* we dwell in him. This means obeying his commandments.

He cannot fully protect us if we treat his dwelling place as a holiday home. Jude v 21 says: *'Keep yourselves in God's love ...'*

We have a part to play.

Deuteronomy 12:30 says that even *inquiring* about other gods can ensnare us. I have seen many young Christians lose or compromise their faith after studying other beliefs at Bible college. They become ensnared and unclear.

The new covenant is equally radical. 1 Corinthians 6:14-15 says: 'For what do righteousness and wickedness have in common? Or what fellowship can light have with darkness? What harmony is there between Christ and Belial?

'Or what does a believer have in common with an unbeliever? What agreement is there between the temple of God and idols?'

Many Christians are blind to the risks, even though the Lord spells them out clearly in the Bible. They flirt with new age philosophies and occult practices, which are cleverly packaged as spiritual, or as manifestations of the Holy Spirit.

If you stray from the truth of God's word, you will blunt the sword of the Spirit. You can't wield God's word, as Jesus did against Satan in the wilderness, if you have compromised it or added to it.

Blunt swords don't harm the devil.

You will also unbuckle the girdle of truth and expose yourself to the enemy's attack, as I discovered several years later.

An epidemic of miscarriages

I went to one church where 80 percent of all pregnancies were resulting in a miscarriage.

It was disturbing to see the effect this had on young couples. Many women feared falling pregnant.

To me, it was clear the enemy was at work. After all, God promised his people in Exodus 20:26: 'There will be no miscarriages or infertility in your land'.

But the enemy will attack God's people if they disobey his commands.

I sought the Lord, and he showed me that the church had publicly compromised on God's word by preaching about the 'Nine Commandments'.

Deuteronomy 4:2 is clear about this: 'You shall not add to the word that I command you, nor take from it.'

The same book spells out the consequences. Deuteronomy 28:15-19 says: 'However, if you do not obey the LORD your God and do not carefully follow all his commands and decrees I am giving you today, all these curses will come on you and overtake you … the fruit of your womb will be cursed.'

I wrote to the leader but received a dismissive reply. I am still mystified how the leadership squared an 80 percent miscarriage rate with God's promise in Exodus 20:26.

Even by worldly standards, the figures were shocking.

In the meantime, many young couples left the church to find a place of safety, and the church declined for a generation as God scattered people due to their leaders' unfaithfulness (see Nehemiah 1:8).

Leaders are shepherds and have a solemn responsibility to protect their sheep. In their desire to be radical, they should never use people to test their latest theological or spiritual experiments.

Sadly, they weren't the first church to discover that playing fast and loose with scripture and the supernatural has consequences.

The word of God stands forever.

CHAPTER 4

Dealing with Enemy Activity

Curses on missionaries

It amazes me how little training some missionaries receive about spiritual warfare before visiting places that are infested with demons.

Some are sent out by churches and organisations that don't even believe in the devil. Others don't believe in the gifts of the Holy Spirit.

No wonder the 'attrition rate' among missionaries is so high. Many good people visit the toughest battlefields without basic training.

I came across my first casualty a year after I became a Christian.

A friend worked for a missionary society and went on a short trip to India. He came back suffering from chronic fatigue.

The doctors could not find anything wrong with him, and prayers for healing had no effect. He spent all day asleep and his doctor signed him off from work.

I met with some friends to pray with him, and God showed me that he had been cursed.

God also told me the name of the person who had cursed him, and how it had happened. To my surprise, the details were accurate.

I did not know anything about curses, so I prayed a rather hesitant prayer to release my friend. Much to my surprise, he jumped off the sofa, completely healed. His energy returned, and he went back to work the next day.

This incident showed me the power of curses, and yet many Christians pay little attention to them, or don't believe in them.

A few years later, a similar thing happened to a woman I knew. She also came back from a mission trip, fatigued, and covered in a horrid skin rash. Again, the medics could not find the cause.

I was asked to pray for her, and once again, God showed me a curse. I broke it in Jesus' name, and she was instantly healed.

Cursed in Nepal

Another time, I noticed a curse resting on a friend who had just returned from a mission trip to Nepal.

He looked really ill, as if he was dying.

I went home and prayed, and God showed me a picture of a flaming arrow made of straw.

I did not know what it meant, so I harnessed the power of the Tree of Knowledge (Google!) to find out.

I discovered that people used flaming straw in religious rituals in the region of Nepal that he had visited.

The following day, he was still fatigued, unwell and had a chronic stomach upset.

I prayed with him and broke the curse. He was healed immediately and went out to a prayer meeting soon afterwards.

Why we minister in pairs

My friend, Norman Page, was once asked to pray for a man who had just returned from the mission field. He was broken and unable to talk properly.

The man had been to Africa but had no concept of the spiritual dangers there.

God showed Norman a picture of a cauldron with someone standing by it. He described what he had seen, and the man indicated that he recognised the individual in the picture. God said to Norman: 'He was cursed by that man.'

Norman prayed and broke the curse, and the man started to speak normally. But suddenly, Norman went cold inside, and his teeth started to chatter.

He managed to tell his pastor: 'Whoever breaks the curse takes it.' Fortunately, the pastor, who had unexpectedly joined the prayer time, understood, and began to pray.

By this time, Norman's jaw had locked, and he became cold and paralysed.

Then he felt like he was on the ceiling, looking down. His soul started to leave his body. Then he saw that the pastor was praying, and his soul returned to his body.

The missionary went home completely freed and healed, while the pastor was wide-eyed in astonishment.

Norman was relieved that the pastor joined the session and learned why Jesus sent his disciples out to work in pairs.

He and I could relate many similar stories. And yet so many mission organisations and churches still don't believe in spiritual warfare.

Bringing light into darkness

I was at a prayer meeting one evening and glanced over at a friend. To my surprise, God showed me four Zulu warriors dancing above her.

Then, the Holy Spirit told me that each warrior represented a curse—one on herself, one on her husband, and one on each of her parents.

The woman and her family were involved in front-line missionary work in Africa, so it was not surprising that they were under attack. I decided not to share anything.

However, at the end of the meeting, my friend approached me.

She had just received a text from someone in Africa, cursing her father. So, I told her what I had 'seen' an hour earlier.

I prayed with her and her husband, and we broke the curse. I also sensed that the enemy was trying to destroy their mission through secrets, and we asked God to expose them.

The following day, another member of the mission team disclosed that she had been cursed as well but had concealed it. However, God quickly turned the curses into blessings.

A picture that told a story

A similar thing happened when I was shown a photo of another missionary from Africa.

As I looked at her photo, God showed me a tribal warrior breaking his spear in half in front of her.

I did some research and discovered that warriors in that part of Africa broke their spears to show that they were ready for hand-to-hand combat. I also saw a picture of some totem poles.

We contacted the missionary, who confirmed that she had been under direct attack from local tribes. Zulu warriors had nailed dead chickens to totem poles on the edge of her property.

We recorded a prayer of protection and deliverance, and she experienced immediate relief.

Satan has plans for your life

Many mission organisations and churches avoid this kind of teaching because they are fearful.

One pastor said to me: 'You might make people afraid.'

But I replied: 'They'll have more reason to be afraid if you don't protect them properly.'

Many groups leave people exposed because they believe that salvation means automatic freedom from demons and curses.

Tragically, their ignorance causes sickness, tragedy and even death to godly, faithful people who go into hostile areas unprepared and ill-equipped.

Of course, the cross is a complete work. Jesus disarmed the devil's powers and authorities and made a public spectacle of them on the cross (Colossians 2:15).

But we must now enforce that victory in faith, by wrestling with a ferocious and deceitful enemy.

If victory were automatic, Joshua and the armies of Israel could have walked into Canaan without lifting a sword. But they spent more than seven years fighting enemies before they conquered the land that was legally theirs.

Sometimes, the devil needs evicting.

Paul told us in 2 Corinthians 2:11 to be alert to his schemes and warned about Satan *outwitting* us. We need to pay attention.

'Schemes' means *organised evildoing,* or a *settled plan.* The Greek words point to an action plan with a clear aim … a plan that is elaborate, systematic, secret, or underhanded, and like planning and directing military operations in a war.

You sometimes need a seer to help expose them.

Satan had a plan for Eve and then Adam in the Garden of Eden, and it worked.

He nearly destroyed Peter's ministry by sifting him to the point where he denied Jesus. He repeatedly stopped Paul from visiting the church in Thessalonica.

He had four plans for Jesus' life—to kill him to tempt him, then divert him and then crucify him. He failed with the three two. And he signed his own death warrant with the third.

Yes, Jesus has won the victory, but we must play our parts. We wear the armour and wield the sword of the Spirit, because we are in a real war.

Satan has plans to accuse you, tempt you, lie to you, divert you, and deceive you. He is committed to making you sick, stealing your finances, destroying your dreams, and killing you if he can. He hates you.

And you won't make it on your own. We are part of the body, and that means seeking out watchmen and watchwomen to help keep us safe.

The apostle Peter knew about spiritual warfare after that sifting by Satan. So, he had good reason to tell us in 1 Peter 5:8: 'Be alert and of sober mind. Your enemy, the devil, prowls around like a roaring lion looking for someone to devour.'

Devour means to *annihilate*. And if you watch wildlife documentaries, you will see that lions pick off the easy targets— the young, the sick, the lonely or the elderly.

The enemy constantly looks for weaknesses.

Ephesians 4:27: 'Do not give the devil a foothold.'

Foothold in Greek means giving space or ground and also refers to being in a 'condition' ... in other words, leading lives that expose us to enemy attack.

What 'condition' are you in?

As I said earlier: be watchful. And then fight that roaring lion by enforcing Jesus' victory, rather than just singing about it.

Seers are often accused of 'looking too much at the devil'. Of course, this is a danger.

But this doesn't mean we blithely carry on as if the devil doesn't exist.

I usually invite missionaries to repent before I break curses over them.

They may need to confess that they have ignored God's word and presumed that he would protect them, instead of utilising their faith and fighting the battle that God has called them to.

CHAPTER 5

How Seers See

God shows seers things in different ways, and in my experience, people may operate more in some realms than others.

These are the ways they 'saw' things in the Bible.

God opens your eyes

When God opens your eyes, you see things differently. You either notice things that other people miss or are aware of things that they cannot see at all.

There's nothing 'spiritual' about this. It's very ordinary, like putting on glasses. Your vision changes.

This anointing doesn't flow all the time. It's God's gift, not ours. I remember feeling really condemned when I met a young man and did not notice that he was an alcoholic and involved in the occult.

It made me realise that seers rely entirely on the Holy Spirit to show them what he wants them to see.

We must recognise when the Holy Spirit is working. If we try to 'produce' something when the anointing is not flowing, we will use human reasoning. That may have its place in some situations but can only go so far and will never resolve spiritual issues.

1 Corinthians 2:14 makes it clear: 'The person without the Spirit does not accept the things that come from the Spirit of God but considers them foolishness, and cannot understand them because they are discerned *only* through the Spirit.'

Dreams, visions, and trances

Christians should expect to see dreams and visions. The prophet Joel said in Joel 2:28: 'And afterward, I will pour out My Spirit on all people. Your sons and daughters will prophesy, your old men will dream dreams, your young men will see visions.' And this was fulfilled when the Holy Spirit was poured out at Pentecost.

Jacob's son Joseph started dreaming God's dreams when he was young (see Genesis 37:1-10), and later, he was able to interpret them (see Genesis 41:1-36).

And his namesake Joseph, Mary's husband, received a warning that saved the young Messiah's life in Matthew 2:13: 'An angel of the Lord appeared to Joseph in a dream and said, 'Get up! Take the child and His mother and flee to Egypt.'

Paul had a vision in Acts 16: 'A vision appeared to Paul in the night: a man of Macedonia was standing and appealing to him, and saying, "Come over to Macedonia and help us."'

God's dreams contain a clear message. They are not mystic and are given for a reason.

It's important to distinguish them from our own dreams. These have no spiritual significance at all, and we should not try to interpret them.

Christians should leave dream interpretation to psychologists and new agers and should only interpret dreams that come from God.

We should also beware an occult activity called oneiromancy, where dreams are used to predict the future. Father God forbids divination, and Jesus told his disciples not to worry about tomorrow.

Trances are not uncommon in scripture. Peter had one during the day. Acts 10:10-11 describes: 'He [Peter] became hungry and wanted something to eat, and while the meal was being prepared, he fell into a trance. He saw heaven opened ...'

But trances experienced by God's people bear no relation to the disconnected, mystic trances experienced by people involved in spiritism and other faiths and beliefs.

When Peter went into a trance, he remained fully engaged. He was able to hear God speak, understand what he said, and reply.

You find the same when Paul refers to being in a trance in Acts 22:17, and the same with John in Revelation 1:17. He initially fell before the Lord as though he was dead. But God didn't leave him in that state.

He touched him, so that he was able to listen, write, use his intelligence, and retain what he was shown.

Beware practices like soaking prayer, that take you into a passive or disconnected state. They are not from God.

Pictures

The most common way of 'seeing' is through God-given pictures in your mind.

For example, Jeremiah 1:11-12 describes: 'The word of the Lord came to me: "What do you see, Jeremiah?"

"I see the branch of an almond tree," I replied. The Lord said to me: "You have seen correctly."'

However, I believe that pictures can be over-used.

I've lost track of the insane prophetic pictures I've heard over the years. And to be fair, I've given a fair few myself.

People have used pictures to describe me as a milkshake, a chopping board, a piece of sandpaper, and both the brake and the accelerator on a car.

And I've heard people earnestly describing camels walking down the high street, people swimming in a sea of chocolate, and jam jars bouncing in a stream.

And then there are the video prophecies ... the tide slowly coming in and never going out, or someone throwing fellow passengers out of a hot air balloon.

And it's even harder when fellow believers nod wisely in agreement when people spout this rubbish, and even say: 'Yes, Lord, amen' rather than asking: 'Have you been at the sherbet again Fred?'

We have conversations in church that would land us with an appointment with the men in white coats in any other situation. It's nothing to do with being a fool for Christ. A lot of it is super-spiritual nonsense.

For example, my friend once saw some King Edward potatoes in the supermarket and believed God was telling him that Prince Edward would one day become king.

At the time of writing, Edward, Duke of Wessex, was 11th in line to the throne and falling down the succession charts every year.

Surprisingly, there are no examples of anyone prophesying with pictures in the New Testament. Pictures were only used by prophets in the Old Testament.

The New Testament only mentions people having trances and visions. But these are separate from the gift of prophecy.

So, we must ask ourselves if the Holy Spirit has introduced this prophetic Pinterest culture, or have we? And what effect has it had on our understanding of God?

Now, Jesus used visual aids like seeds, yeast, flowers, and birds when he taught, to make things easier to understand, or to strengthen their impact.

For instance, he used a picture of someone with a plank in their eye and contrasted it with someone else with a speck in theirs. The meaning was obvious.

But imagine someone bringing that picture to your prayer meeting: 'I see a picture of a big piece of wood sticking out of someone's eye. And there's a speck of sawdust in someone else's eye.

'Doris, the wood in your eye describes the way Jesus, the carpenter, is going to chisel you into something useful.

'And Cyril, you feel like a speck of sawdust. But even a tiny speck can be useful to God for his own glory.'

Hmmm.

Some picture prophecies often obscure God's word by making it mystic. So, I advise people: 'Just tell it like it is.'

I mean, why give someone a picture of an empty cup, when you can say: 'Mavis, you feel empty'. And why give them a picture of a dog on a lead when you can tell them: 'God is restraining you.'

People often use pictures because they don't know the scriptures. And I'm not saying this is wrong. Far from it. God works within our faith, but scriptures have more power.

Sometimes, however, the Spirit expresses a word as a picture to give it impact, or to communicate with someone in a way they understand.

For example, I was part of a group that was asked to pray for the safe delivery of a baby.

My son Jake had a picture of a baby made of glass, and this enabled us to pray more precisely, knowing that the child would need very delicate handling during delivery.

It transpired that it was a difficult birth, but the baby was born safely.

So, pictures have their place, and even when they appear silly to us, they may have a powerful significance to the people we give them to.

But pictures often fit into a culture where prophecies just feed people's souls and their self-centredness, rather than shape them for a sacrificial walk of self-denial.

What to do with what you see

Seeing is different from 'hearing' from God:

You *hear* one thing at a time, but you may *see* many things at once.

As a result, seers work differently to prophets.

Prophets hear God's word and then deliver it.

In contrast, seers see many things, but usually do nothing other than pray. Some people struggle to understand this. This illustration might help.

Imagine you are walking down the street. You see a man on a bike, a lamppost, a parked car, a pensioner dropping his wallet, some litter on the pavement, a traffic warden issuing a ticket and a lot else besides.

You feel compassion for the pensioner who dropped his wallet, so you pick it up for him.

So, although you saw many things, you only acted on one of them. You could have argued with the traffic warden or picked up the litter. But you didn't tackle everything you saw. Just the instance where someone would suffer without your intervention.

This is how seers work. They should only act when the Holy Spirit prompts them. And, as I said in an earlier chapter, this prompting usually comes when people ask them for help. Even then, seers might not share everything they have seen.

So, a seer must always ask for God's wisdom. They must respond to the Spirit, not to the person's need, or their own need to be the 'person with a revelation'.

These guidelines may help you process what you see:

1. Pause and ask God

A seer must work in harmony with God. Ephesians 5:17 says: 'Don't act thoughtlessly but *try to find out* and do whatever the Lord wants you to.'

Finding out takes time and it's best to be cautious. Mistakes can cause pain and have a profound effect on other people's lives.

I once 'saw' that a woman who was dying of cancer was affected by a curse caused by worshipping another god. The following day, the Holy Spirit clearly told me to phone her brother and arrange to pray for her.

I didn't, and she died two days later. I was broken with self-recrimination and guilt. Father reassured me that her healing depended on him, not me. But I still carry the wound of 'getting it wrong'.

2. *Test what you see*

It's best to weigh what you see with someone else before you pass it on.

If it relates to a person, then share it with someone who knows them and cares about them.

And if it's about a church, weigh it with the leader and never discuss it with anyone else, even 'for prayer.' Prayers like this are often super-spiritual gossip. Once you share your insights with a leader, you have done your job, and the rest is up to them.

Don't expect a good reaction. Prophets and seers are rarely heard by God's people. Jonah was one of the few who saw a good response—but that was from gentiles!

THE PATH OF THE SEER

3. *Write things down and wait*

Timing is important. Jesus waited four days before raising Lazarus from the dead. He left it until the third watch of the night to rescue the disciples in the storm.

I note the things I see, so I don't forget them, with the person's name and the date, and how the insight came to me.

Then I wait for God to show me when and if to use them. Most of them remain unshared.

Habakkuk 2:2 gives some good advice: 'Write the vision; make it plain on tablets, so he may run who reads it. For still, the vision awaits its appointed time; it hastens to the end - it will not lie. If it seems slow, wait for it; it will surely come; it will not delay.'

Everything God shows us has an 'appointed time'. Our job is to wait until he tells us.

A person may not be ready for healing, repentance, or change. This is why Jesus told his disciples in John

16:12: 'There is so much more I want to tell you, but you can't bear it now.'

Jesus saw the needs in everyone he saw, but mainly helped people who came to him in faith.

He knew about Judas' thieving, but did not mention it. He just showed him unconditional love and created opportunities for him to come clean. He didn't.

Jesus knew Peter had a problem with fear. Peter didn't. He clearly believed his own claim in Matthew 26:35: 'Even if I have to die with you, I will never disown you.'

But Jesus did nothing until Peter's heart was right. Peter had to discover his own weakness by denying Jesus after his arrest. Then Jesus was able to bring healing and restoration during that beach barbeque.

Acting hastily can cause unnecessary hurt. The wisest option is to pray and say nothing unless someone's actions are damaging to other people.

CHAPTER 6

Miracles in Marriages

An amazing reconciliation

It is rewarding when God allows you to see something that leads to a miracle.

One morning I visited a church in northeast London, and during the worship, the Holy Spirit drew my attention to a man sitting on one side of the meeting. Later, he showed me a woman sitting on the other side.

I did not know either of them, but 'saw' that they should be together.

I nervously shared my impressions with the pastor, and he excitedly called the two people over. I wondered what I was getting myself into!

It transpired that they were married but separated. Their relationship was over.

But they were so encouraged that God saw them 'together', they decided to give their relationship another chance. They eventually got back together.

Demons trembled ... eventually

Another couple contacted me because their marriage would not work, even though they clearly loved one another.

Every conversation ended in an argument, and everything they did together ended with problems.

God showed me they were under the influence of a hex, a harmful magic spell created by witches. It transpired that the woman had been previously married to a warlock.

A group of friends and I confronted some evil forces in Jesus' name for several weeks, and eventually, we saw a breakthrough. The couple's relationship was quickly and wonderfully restored.

CHAPTER 7

Physical Healings

The role of the seer in miracles

Some Christians receive miraculous healing with one prayer. But many don't because there is a blockage. This is especially the case these days, where Christians have compromised on God's word.

A seer may help to find the issue that is obstructing healing.

Jesus saw root issues

Jesus frequently saw the root causes of people's sickness and exposed them.

He saw that the man at the pool of Bethesda had given up hope (John 5:1-9).

The passage says that the blind, the lame and the paralysed were by the pool, but refers to this guy as an invalid. And the Greek word invalid in this context meant that he was ill, or more tellingly, weak.

In verse 8, we are told that the man was 'cured', and the Greek word here means made whole, made sound, and restored. This is a different word used to describe Jesus's other miracles.

So, this man received more than physical healing. He needed wholeness, and eight words from Jesus were enough to put him back on his feet.

Jesus also saw that he had been paralysed by sin (John 5:14). But he did not address this until the man was back on his feet again.

Another time, he saw that a man was paralysed by sin and guilt (Matthew 9:1-8).

And he discerned that a man who shouted at him in a synagogue had an unclean spirit (Mark 1: 23-28).

The lame walk

I once ministered to a young woman who could only walk a few faltering steps with the aid of a walker.

I saw that she had a wounded spirit and prayed for healing. Next time we met, she was walking normally and unaided. She told me that the bones in her spine had been crumbling.

This made sense. Proverbs 17:22 says: 'A cheerful heart is good medicine, but a crushed spirit dries up the bones.' Bone problems can be caused by a crushed or broken spirit, or by envy (see Proverbs 14:30).

I also prayed for an elderly lady who could only walk four paces. God showed me that she had a wounded spirit.

A few days later, she walked more than a mile round her local shops and was still walking normally two years later.

An end to decades of infirmity

A woman in her late 60s experienced the most amazing series of miracles over several months.

She suffered from aspiration pneumonia and hadn't been out of hospital for more than 17 consecutive days since around 2005.

I prayed with her over the phone after I 'saw' the root cause – freemasonry in the family line. We broke some curses, and God healed her. However, the doctors were unable to clear the fluid on her lungs.

God reminded me how Moses drained water out of a rock by striking it. So, I 'struck' her lungs with the Jesus' sceptre of authority, and they cleared completely. She has not been readmitted to hospital for breathing problems since then.

The Holy Spirit also healed her asthma. Her next peak flow test that her breathing strength had doubled.

However, she was still in chronic pain from prolapsed and herniated discs, osteoarthritis, osteoporosis, trapped nerves in her spine from neck down, and worsening stenosis. She could only walk a few paces and used opioids to combat the pain.

God show me a strong man influencing her life, so I bound it according to Mark 3:27. She did not know I had prayed for her. The following day, she woke up free of pain and discovered she had been healed. She walked unaided around a farm and climbed a flight of stairs at her church, much to the Vicar's surprise.

She gradually stopped her medication—38 tablets a day—and travelled on a train for the first time in 18 years. God also healed her of mental illness. She was discharged after 53 years' treatment.

She even started applying for jobs because she lost her carers and disability allowances.

Later, she was healed of a hernia that she had suffered with for 28 years and regained the sight in one eye. She had been blind since was she a little girl.

Healed from chronic pain

I prayed for another woman who had suffered from costochondritis for many years and was taking opioids to combat chronic pain.

She was unable to drive and had to be cared for at home.

God showed me several root issues and healed her. She is now pain free, able to drive and living a normal life again.

Miracle babies

The scriptures show that there are many causes of childlessness. In some cases, the situation won't change unless the spiritual roots are dealt with.

God sometimes closes a woman's womb, and only he can open it again (Gen 30:22).

I was asked to pray for one couple who had been trying for a baby for several years. I saw that the wife was under a curse. We prayed and broke it.

She became pregnant the following month. She and her husband now have three adult children.

More recently, a Christian couple came to see me, and before they arrived, God gave me a vision of them with young children.

I was hesitant to share it with virtual strangers, but over dinner, they told me that they had been trying for a baby for 18 years.

I gave them the word, and we prayed. The following week that she discovered she was pregnant.

Burdens lifted

One lady had bad pain in her shoulder, and I 'saw' that she was carrying a burden about her estranged daughter.

We prayed, and her shoulder was instantly healed. She even cancelled a doctor's appointment the following day.

Have your cake and eat it

God once showed me in a healing meeting that a young man was suffering from an eating disorder. He suffered chronic pain if he ate anything containing flour.

I asked the Holy Spirit to heal him, and he went home and ate an entire sponge cake without any repercussions.

At the same meeting, God showed me that a woman had agoraphobia. He prayed, and she started going out and living a normal life.

A life saved through intercession

My team and I were asked to pray for a woman who was dangerously ill. Several internal organs became misplaced after a hernia twisted itself around her inside.

The growth was two feet wide and stretched across her body.

She faced a major operation of between 12 and 15 hours, where a team of five consultants would attempt to reposition her heart, lungs, and kidneys. She also needed a colostomy.

The medics only gave her a 50 percent chance of survival. They said that if she lived, she would be placed in an induced coma and faced a long spell in intensive care, followed by months in hospital.

However, God had other ideas, and the Holy Spirit led us in prayer and spiritual warfare for six months.

To begin with, healing was well beyond our faith, but God reminded me that faith came by hearing his word.

So, I searched the scriptures, as I believe that God's word sheds light on every human condition.

He steered me towards Psalm 139:13-16, and its well-known insights about God's deep involvement in our conception and formation in the womb.

It says: 'For you created my inmost being; you knit me together in my mother's womb.'

These words jumped out at me: 'For you created my *inmost being.*'

When I studied this phrase in Hebrew, I discovered that *inmost being* refers to the kidneys and other internal organs.

I also learned that the Jewish people saw a spiritual connection between people's internal organs and their 'inner man'. The heart, of course, is the most obvious example.

We prayed and interceded, and God pointed me to Hebrews 12:15: 'See to it that no one falls short of the grace of God and that no *bitter root* grows up to cause trouble and defile many.'

Did this lady have a bitter root growing inside her? I asked her family, who confirmed that she was very bitter, and so we started praying about it.

The lady did not even know that we were praying. But Father allowed us to stand in the gap and confess her sin on her behalf.

The next breakthrough came when God showed me Psalm 73:21: 'Then I realised that my heart was bitter, and I was *all torn up inside.*'

This was what was happening to this dear lady. Other translations emphasised the link between internal organs and emotional pain.

The Holman Christian Standard Bible said: 'When I became embittered, and my innermost being was wounded ...' and the New English Translation translated it thus: 'Yes, my spirit was bitter, and my insides felt sharp pain.'

The Aramaic Bible in Plain English was even more graphic: 'And I am troubled; my heart and my kidneys rage against me.'

We intensified our prayers, and God repeatedly delayed the operation to bring emotional healing and reconciliation to the lady and her family. Her bitterness disappeared.

His timing was perfect.

Eventually, the lady received the go-ahead for surgery. She said an emotional goodbye to her parents and children, not knowing if she would see them again. The surgeons privately admitted they were afraid to operate.

I was in Jerusalem that day with Norman and Sheila Page.

We unexpectedly found ourselves standing outside the Church of the Flagellation in the Via Dolorosa, while she was having the operation.

This was where Jesus was 'pierced for our transgressions and wounded for our iniquities ... and by his stripes, we are healed' (1 Peter 2:24). It seemed that God had led us to the best place to pray.

We also filmed a prayer based on 'By his stripes, she is healed' and sent it to the lady's mother on WhatsApp.

Later that day, we were stunned to discover what God had done.

The surgeons found that her condition was better than they had expected.

The operation took six hours, less than half the time expected.

She did not need a colostomy, and did not have to be placed in an induced coma.

She got out of bed and sat in a chair the next day, left intensive care a few days later, and was sent home in just 12 days.

She even travelled to London by train two weeks later.

So, God dealt with the physical and emotional roots, making the operation simpler. It was a complete success.

To this day, she still doesn't know the full story ... only that we prayed for her.

I slowly realised that although Jesus does instant miracles, others need persistent prayer, revelation, and spiritual warfare. The ability to 'see' was fundamental.

'Be clean ...'

Another guy asked me to pray for chronic acne. God showed me a curse due to generational sin, and we broke it. The Holy Spirit told me to say: 'Be clean,' just like Jesus said to people with leprosy.

I met him a month later and did not recognise him – his skin was clear and smooth. There was no trace of acne.

Healed from cancer

Another time, I was driving home from a meeting late at night, when a friend told me his mum was dying of cancer.

I was too tired to show much interest. I just wanted to go home. But I grudgingly mumbled a prayer based on what I saw and thought no more about it.

But she discovered the following day that God had healed her. I was shocked. She was too! The Lord reminded me that *he* is the healer.

A little boy healed

I was contacted by the parents of a little boy who wouldn't eat solid foods or drink properly. He either ignored food, or grimaced and shivered when he saw it and was unable to chew, eat, or swallow.

The medics were concerned that he had a sensory disorder.

We prayed, and God showed us that he had become fearful in his mother's womb.

We released him from fear, and his parents saw an improvement the next day. He began eating more normally and drank from his beaker for the first time.

During the following months, he started eating solids and developed a healthy appetite.

CHAPTER 8

Why Christians Aren't Healed

I have prayed for many Christians who don't get healed because they are trapped by their theology.

They think salvation means automatic freedom from demons, curses, and generational issues.

But Joshua and his people battled for at least seven years to conquer the Promised Land, even though it was theirs. Why?

God explains in Exodus 23:29: 'I will not drive them [your enemies] out *in a single year,* because the land would become desolate and the wild animals too numerous for you.'

The story of the prodigal son shows we would not cope if God gave us our inheritance in one go.

If he did, parts of our lives would become desolate, and wild animals—the enemy—would take advantage.

Yes, the cross was a complete work. But salvation is not automatic. It must be worked out with fear and trembling (Philippians 2:12). 'Worked out' means labour until you finish. It's a process.

What blocks healing?

The Bible gives several reasons why people aren't healed. A seer may have insight into individual situations.

These are the most common obstacles:

1.   Breaking the covenant.

Breaking of bread comes with a health warning.

Paul wrote in 1 Corinthians 11: 29-31: 'For those who eat and drink without discerning the body of Christ, eat and drink judgement on themselves.

'That is why many among you are weak and sick, and a number of you have fallen asleep.'

The new covenant provided forgiveness for our sins and healing for our diseases. Jesus sealed it by shedding his blood. And he identified his blood through communion.

But we exclude ourselves from the new covenant if we take communion with unconfessed sin, unrepentant hearts, unforgiveness, or if we are out of relationship with another Christian.

The bread, which was broken for our healing, then works the opposite way around and brings sickness.

Similarly, the cup no longer brings forgiveness and cleansing, but condemnation, judgement, weakness, sickness, and early death.

We have a choice. Communion can either affirm the new covenant and bring us healing and forgiveness. Or it can condemn us to judgement and sickness.

Broken relationships inflict weakness, sickness, and death on those involved – even entire congregations. Sometimes, whole communities are plagued with sickness because churches are at war with one another.

It's easy to get absorbed in the communion ceremony and forget that the body of Christ is also the person sitting next to you.

Now, I'm not saying all sickness is due to sin. But for me, if I'm ill, I go to God and ask: 'What's wrong?'

2.   *No anointing by elders*

James 5:14 says: 'Is anyone among you sick? Let them call the elders of the church to pray over them and anoint them with oil in the name of the Lord.

'And the prayer offered in faith will make the sick person well; the Lord will raise them up.'

These verses speak for themselves. If you don't have elders who are willing to anoint you with oil, then you should find a church that has.

3.   *Lack of confession*

James 5 also says that healing involves confessing our sins to one another.

This isn't surprising, as the Bible frequently refers to sin and sickness together. Jesus sometimes dealt with both.

Few Christians confess their sins to one another and are ill as a result.

Tragically, I've seen many cases where people prefer sickness, and early death, to transparency. They fear the consequences of walking in God's light.

James doesn't tell us to confess our sin to everyone. Just to someone. If you can't find someone trustworthy, then find a spiritual director, a Christian counsellor, or a priest.

4.   *Unforgiveness*

If you are tormented by illness, you may need to ask yourself: 'Is there anyone I haven't forgiven?'

Jesus said in the parable of the unmerciful servant (Matt 18:21-35) that his Father arranges for unforgiving believers to be tortured. Ouch!

This cuts across the concept of God being a daddy who hands out blessings like sweeties.

Jesus said in Matthew 6: 15: 'If you do not forgive others their trespasses, neither will your Father forgive your trespasses.'

This explains why some people feel guilty all the time. In God's sight, they *are* guilty. Unforgiveness then opens the door to physical, mental, or emotional torment.

I've prayed for people who prefer to suffer cancer, wasting diseases, and mental illness, rather than forgive someone.

Forgiveness isn't easy. The hurt, abuse, and damage that people inflict on us is very real.

You aren't responsible for their actions. But you are responsible for forgiving them. Or not.

THE PATH OF THE SEER

They may not deserve your forgiveness. But you don't deserve God's. Neither do I.

5.   *Curses*

The Bible says that sickness can be caused by a curse.

Some Bible-believing Christians struggle to accept this. They also struggle to get healed!

In Deuteronomy 28, God warned his people that they would be cursed with wasting diseases, fever, inflammation, incurable boils, tumours, festering sores and itching, madness, blindness, and confusion if they disobeyed his commands.

This list covers most afflictions in society today.

He also said he would visit the fathers' iniquities on their children and their children's children ... 'to the third and the fourth generation of those who hate him.'

We should not take these verses lightly.

Some people say that a Christian cannot be under a curse because curses were broken by Jesus on the cross. And they are right. Galatians 3:13 says: 'Christ redeemed us from the curse of the law by becoming a curse for us.'

But God's promises must be possessed by faith.

Not all sickness is caused by a curse. But if your condition hasn't responded to prayer, then you should seek then input of a seer.

6.   *Lack of submission to God*

We sometimes want God to heal us on our terms. So, we remain sick.

Jesus healed people in strange ways. He put his fingers in one man's ears, rubbed mud in another man's eyes, and told a paralysed man to stop sinning.

In the Old Testament, Naaman, chief of the king's army, had leprosy. Elisha told him to bathe in the River Jordan seven times. But Naaman angrily resisted and set out his own T&Cs.

His pride was stronger than his desire to get better.

We're sometimes the same. We want Jesus to heal us 'respectably' through prayer. But Jesus never prayed for anyone to get healed.

Perhaps you don't want to be healed in public, or don't like people laying hands on you.

Your attitudes may reveal the reason why you don't get better.

Jesus will heal you on his terms. It's your chance to prove that he's Lord.

7.   *Evil spirits*

Jesus healed people whose health was affected by demons.

He delivered a boy from epilepsy (see Luke 9:37ff). He released a woman from a spirit of infirmity (see Luke 13:10ff).

But he didn't pray for them. He tackled the evil spirits.

If your sickness is caused by a demon, you won't get better unless it is kicked out in Jesus' name.

Some Christians say they can't 'have' a demon. This is true. They cannot be 'possessed' if Jesus is truly their Lord.

But the Greek word for 'possession' refers to influence, not ownership. Demons can influence a believer's health.

The woman with the spirit of infirmity was a believer, a synagogue attender, and had such strong faith that Jesus called her a daughter of Abraham. But the enemy had still afflicted her with a back problem for 18 years.

Faith on its own is not always enough. You may have faith that Jesus has overcome the enemy, but you still need to evict him in Jesus' name.

Not all sicknesses are caused by demons. But some are. And if God has not healed you, then ask a seer or someone with the gift of discernment to pray with you.

CHAPTER 9

Face to Face with the Enemy

Confronting evil

Jesus gave us the authority to confront and expose evil spirits, and our churches and ministries will be ineffective, unless we use it.

And so, the Holy Spirit gives us the gift of discernment, as human reasoning dethrones God and leads to human conclusions.

1 Corinthians 2:14 says: 'The person without the Spirit does not accept the things that come from the Spirit of God, but considers them foolishness, and cannot understand them because they are discerned only through the Spirit.'

Only God can impart the gift of discernment. It cannot be activated, and it is risky and contrary to scripture to try to.

Discernment is about perception, and using our spiritual senses to discern five types of spirits:

- Holy Spirit.
- Angels of God.
- Fallen angels.
- Evil spirits (demons).
- The human spirit.

Jesus showed how discernment worked in Matthew 16:22. It says: 'But Peter took him aside and began to reprimand him for saying such things. "Heaven forbid, Lord," he said. "This will never happen to you!"'

Jesus turned to Peter and said: 'Get away from me, Satan! You are a dangerous trap to me. You are seeing things merely from *a human point of view*, not from God's.'

Jesus discerned that Satan was trying to trap him through Peter's well-intentioned advice.

In Acts 16:17, Paul was on a mission in Macedonia, and a young fortune teller followed him and his team, shouting: 'These men are servants of the Most High God, who are telling you the way to be saved.'

Some people would have rejoiced in her proclamation and signed her up for an Alpha Course. But Paul discerned a spirit of divination and cast it out.

The gift of discernment is absent in many churches today, which is why they embrace practices that God describes as detestable.

They are flippant about the new age and the occult, and compromise by getting involved in witchcraft through things like Harry Potter and demonology through Pokémon and elves.

I know churches that hold Harry Potter film nights, and one that held a Pokémon picnic.

The enemy uses fantasy creatures such as dragons, elves, pixies, fairies, and leprechauns to make demons acceptable to children. They would be terrified if they saw what those demons really looked like.

These practices allow the devil to gain a toehold into young lives. It's ironic that Vicars and Sunday school teachers pass safeguarding checks, but then put children at risk by foolishly exposing them to the powers of darkness.

Many children these days are as proficient as witches in cursing people. Some curse their parents and teachers, and these curses are not fantasy.

If kids play cops and robbers, they use pretend guns. But there's no such thing as 'pretend' occult. A curse is a curse. There is no fantasy equivalent.

In addition, practices like channelling, two-way journaling and activations have their roots in the new age and the occult. So have many activities that people attribute to the Holy Spirit.

We need discernment now more than any other time in church history.

Delivered from a curse by witches

If you are unsure about the dangers of the occult, maybe these true stories will convince you.

A divorced man came for prayer, suffering from strange pains in his head. The doctors had been unable to diagnose the cause.

God showed me that his ex-wife was a witch and had laid a curse on him. He confirmed that she was now in a coven.

When we prayed, my house filled with the vile smell of rotting corpses.

But when God released the man from the curse, the stench was replaced by the sweet aroma of the Lord, and his pain disappeared immediately.

Satan is a merciless foe

One family was heavily and persistently cursed by a powerful coven based in southeast London. They endured months of relentless attack upon their health, finances, marriage, children, and safety.

And there wasn't a happy ending. The wife collapsed and died one evening when her heart stopped. She was fit and healthy and had no history of heart trouble.

She had been cursed, and the husband was left alone with three young boys, including a baby.

So, does that mean Jesus was not Lord? No, not at all. Jesus won a complete victory over Satan and the forces of darkness. But weak and fallible people like me and you must enforce it. And we sometimes make mistakes, lack wisdom, or disobey God's word.

You are no match for the devil

Don't engage with the devil. Jesus didn't. He just quoted scripture to him or told him to leave. Why try to do better?

1 John 4:4 says: 'The one who is in you is greater than the one who is in the world.'

Re-read it. Who is greater? Not you!

And, although Jesus is the Lord, Satan wins some battles.

Yes, Jesus has won the victory. But we must play our parts and appropriate it by faith.

We wear armour and wield the sword of the Spirit, because we are in a real war. That's why Paul used the word 'wrestle' in Ephesians 6. It means 'a struggle, fight, conflict, or contest'.

Jesus has won the ultimate Game of Thrones. He is sitting on a throne at God's right hand, having ridiculed and shamed the hordes of hell on the cross (Colossians 2:5).

But he also warned that Satan comes to kill, steal, and destroy, and maybe he's tried these tactics with you, like he has done with me.

I do not fear the enemy, but I respect him.

He was confident enough to tempt Jesus using scriptures. He roams heaven and has seen God face to face. He knows how to bring each of us down if we give him the opportunity.

So, I get nervous when Christians throw down the gauntlet to the devil. He'll readily accept the challenge. And if you fight him in your own strength, or without proper training and people around you, you will suffer.

You are not strong enough to fight a demon or an evil spirit. No one is. You can only fight the powers of darkness with the authority of the name of Jesus.

And his authority isn't a method. It's a lifestyle.

Legitimate authority

Authority in the name of Jesus is not enough on its own.

You need legitimate authority to deliver people from the enemy's grip. That means mastering the devil in your own life.

This doesn't mean you have to be perfect. You never will be until you get to heaven. But you should be able to master the sin that crouches at your door (Genesis 4:7) and confess your sin to God and others regularly.

I once heard about a man who raised his wife from the dead. His friends were not surprised, as the miracle reflected his walk with God. You can't turn faith or authority on and off like a tap. They are a part of your lifestyle.

The seven sons of Sceva discovered in Acts 19:7-10 that reciting 'in the name of Jesus' is not effective if the enemy doesn't 'know' you. Legitimate authority is cultivated by faith, experience, and by knowing and using God's word,

I remember a man telling his pastor that he was going to raise a friend from the dead. There was an embarrassed silence, and the pastor asked him: 'But you've got a bad cold.'

The man looked puzzled. Then the pastor said: 'You won't have faith to raise the dead if you haven't got faith for God to heal your cold.' Fair point!

I was once ministering at a healing meeting when a demon-possessed man ran at me, ready to break a chair over my head.

I commanded the spirits to halt in Jesus name, and they did, much to my relief. It's occasions like this when you discover how much legitimate authority you really have!

Destroyed by curses

In 2016, I met two families in different churches and on different occasions.

Both times, God showed me they had been cursed by witches and had hexes laid on them and their children.

Their stories were similar. Their children suffered devastating afflictions and traumas.

Both couples had prayed on a hilltop renowned for centuries for witchcraft, Satanism, and other occult practices.

Some places are infested with demons, and Christians should only engage the enemy there if God tells them to.

You need faith and experience for this type of spiritual warfare.

Apart from anything else, we must ask ourselves: 'What's the point of establishing God's kingdom up on a hill?'

Jesus told us to go and make disciples of all nations, not to shout at the devil on a hillside.

Neither Jesus nor the New Testament churches did anything like this. Paul just preached the gospel on Mars Hill (Acts 17:22ff), which was a centre of idolatry. This was genuine territorial warfare.

Now, some people would say that these families should have been immune because God was their shield and their defender.

This is true, but also shows a frightening lack of understanding of God's word.

Jesus said in Luke 14:31: 'Suppose a king is about to go to war against another king. Won't he first sit down and consider whether he is able with 10,000 men to oppose the one coming against him with 20,000?

'If he is not able, he will send a delegation while the other is still a long way off and will ask for terms of peace.'

The mighty King David usually asked God if he should go into battle. We should do the same. I tend to rush into spiritual battles without 'enquiring of the Lord.' It's easy to use presumption, rather than faith. But battles belong to the Lord.

We should also take advice before engaging the enemy. Proverbs 20:18 says: 'Plans are established by seeking advice; so, if you wage war, obtain guidance.'

In the firing line

There was a period when my family was under a severe attack.

The enemy was relentlessly destroying our physical and emotional health, our relationships, and our finances. It was serious.

I had suffered a physical and mental breakdown and nearly went bankrupt several times.

But a man had a word of knowledge for me at a conference. He said that we had been cursed by covens in the east end of London, where I used to help lead a church.

I asked him: 'OK, but what do I do?'

He replied: 'Bless those who curse you.'

So, my family did just that. We spent several hours in prayer and spiritual warfare, enforcing Jesus' victory and claiming back the ground that the enemy had stolen.

It worked. We saw immediate results in some areas. Others took longer. But eventually, we enforced Jesus' victory. I reclaimed my health and prosperity, and God restored the remnants of my ministry.

The healing was completed when a man with a national prophetic ministry came up to me at a meeting. He knew nothing about my situation but said: 'God wants you to know it was not your fault. He does not hold you to blame, but honours you for standing firm.'

This episode reminded me that we really are in a war. Praying and 'gazing on Jesus' is essential, but not always enough on its own.

If it were, Jesus wouldn't have told us to cast out demons and bind the strong men, and Paul would not have written his 'we wrestle not' passage in Ephesians 6.

Fight the enemy in the right place

Sometimes the enemy gets you on the run, and it's hard to find victory. This may be because you are fighting him in the wrong place.

In 1 Kings 20: 23, the king of Aram attacked the Israelites and lost.

So, his officials advised him: 'Their gods are gods of the hills. That is why they were too strong for us. But if we fight them on the plains, surely we will be stronger than they.'

The enemy is a shrewd tactician and will try to drag us down to his level. He knows he can't touch us when we are seated on the high ground—with Christ in heavenly places.

So, he harasses us, lies to us, and wears us out through accusations, condemnation and temptation, so that we leave the place of prayer, praise, and faith.

Jesus wants us to fight in the heavenly places. This is where victories are won.

One guy told me: 'You focus too much on the devil. Just look at Jesus.'

But how can we be alert to the devil (see 1 Peter 5:8) and aware of his plans (see 2 Cor 11) if we don't discern what he is doing?

I did not have the heart to point out to this guy that his marriage was a sham, his son was involved in crime, and his wife was sick and depressed.

Perhaps if he had focused more on the enemy's attacks on his own family, Jesus' victory over the powers of darkness would have been more than a theory.

CHAPTER 10

Emotional Healing

Beauty restored

God loves to heal people's emotional or psychological problems. Our society clearly does not have the resources to meet people's deepest needs.

When Jesus healed a woman who had suffered from heavy bleeding for many years (see Matthew 9: 20-22), he didn't just cure her physical condition. The Greek text uses the word *sesōken,* which means he brought her into divine safety, restored her and gave her an ongoing recovery.

True salvation means that God can heal us in spirit, soul, and body.

I once met a girl at a youth meeting. She was unkempt and wearing shabby clothes and told me her friends taunted her, saying that she was ugly.

I said to her: 'God says you are a really beautiful princess.' She looked at me as though I was mad and walked off.

A year later, I was at the same conference and a radiant, attractive girl came up to me. 'You spoke to me last year,' she said.

It was the same girl. She told me that God's word had transformed her. He changed her thinking and healed her low self-image, and the reasons for it. The word of the Lord *is* living and active!

This sullen, withdrawn, and unattractive teenager was now a vivacious and beautiful young woman who was wholeheartedly pursuing Jesus, her Saviour.

Another girl at the same conference suffered from epileptic fits and was on strong medication. She had a one while I was preaching, but God showed me that she had faked it to attract attention.

I spoke to her later, and she confessed that she staged fits if she was out of the limelight.

We prayed, and she confessed her deceitfulness. God healed her deep craving for attention, and she did not have a fit—real or fake—again.

A question resolved

Another time, I met a young man, and I 'saw' he had the word 'WHY?' written across his face.

He asked me to pray for him later, and he started crying out: 'Why? Why? Why?'

It turned out that his parents had rejected him when he was young, and he never understood why. He was deeply wounded.

The Holy Spirit delivered him from a spirit of rejection and brought emotional healing. His question was resolved by knowing that Jesus accepted him unconditionally.

I have seen 'writing on people's faces' several times. Once, I noticed a man in a church meeting had 'ADULTERY' written across his forehead. Tragically, it was true.

Healed of anorexia

I was once asked to pray for a girl who was expected to die from anorexia, unless she started eating within a few days.

Her family had run out of options, and counselling and psychiatric care had not worked.

God showed me that she had no intention of improving. She wanted to die. He also showed me why.

She admitted I was right, and the Holy Spirit healed her. She started eating again the same day, and eventually made a full recovery.

An end to torment

An American woman came to see me. She was suffering from an eating disorder and insomnia. She was tormented each night by disturbing images of faces.

The Holy Spirit showed me that her soul had been stolen by a man who was involved in the occult.

She confirmed that she had formed a friendship with a man who had taken over her life.

He controlled her mind, her finances, her diary, everything. We prayed, and God freed her so that she was able to go home and make her own decisions.

Freed from heroin addiction

I was once asked to pray for a girl who was addicted to heroin. Her face was gaunt and pale, and God showed me that she carried deep pain after being abandoned by her mother.

We prayed for healing and deliverance, and the Holy Spirit instantly released from her addiction. She started smiling, her eyes shone, and the colour came back to her cheeks. She was able to quit drugs without any withdrawal symptoms.

An orphan healed

Norman Page had a breakthrough with a German boy who came to his home for prayer.

Norman saw a picture of a screen and in the centre, in big letters were the words: *Ein Blatt.*

The boy said they meant *a piece of paper* and started sobbing deeply. His groans shook his whole body. Eventually, he composed himself, and Norman asked him what had happened.

God had shown the boy a vision of a room with a woman sitting at a desk, writing on a piece of paper.

He realised it was his mother. God showed him she was writing a letter consigning him to an orphanage because his family could not afford to keep him.

The experience had broken him, but God healed him. His frown turned into a smile, and slumped, relaxed, and happy into his chair as the tension left.

An end to mental torment

One lady asked for prayer after struggling with her thoughts. I saw a vision of her hanging things up in a wardrobe and told her that God was inviting her to hang up things from her past.

She was shocked because she had re-arranged her wardrobe that week and understood exactly what God meant. She said later: 'I was struggling mentally but woke up today feeling so well rested and so much better.'

Another time, I was praying for a woman and saw a vision of several clocks on a table. I told her: 'You're driven by time.'

She was so surprised, as she had a tablecloth on her dining room covered with images of clocks. And God set her free from the mental and emotional issues that had troubled her for a long time.

The Holy Spirit certainly knows how to attract people's attention.

CHAPTER 11

Weighing Spiritual Manifestations

Lack of discernment damages lives

S adly, few church leaders have the biblical understanding or the discernment to test spiritual manifestations.

Some attribute all strange behaviour to the Holy Spirit. As a result, weird and ungodly practices have become embedded in church life, and more seriously, people are placed at risk and their needs are not always met. The input of a seer is essential.

I have been in meetings where people have howled in distress from a wounded spirit, while some undiscerning deliverance enthusiast tried to cast out a demon.

So, these unfortunate folks had to endure a potentially harmful 'deliverance' while their problems remained untouched.

I have frequently seen people being 'slain in the spirit' when they had a spirit of death or a spirit of passivity. A wrong diagnosis produces the wrong treatment.

There is no record in the Bible of anyone falling backwards under the power of the Holy Spirit.

People fell *forwards* in the presence of God the Father, as Joshua did (Joshua 5:14).

In Revelation 1:17, John fell before the Lord as though he was dead, but God did not let him stay that way.

He touched him so that he was able to listen, write, use his intelligence, and retain what he was shown.

Christian spirituality should never make you passive because passivity creates an environment where we can be prone to the influence of evil spirits.

Signs and blunders

The Toronto revival was a true work of God and one of the biggest outpourings of the Holy Spirit in history.

But I was shocked at the lack of discernment both during it and since. Many good leaders kissed their bibles and their brains, goodbye.

In some revival meetings, I saw people jumping up and down, rolling on the floor, shadow boxing, or running on the spot.

Others shouted, roared, barked, snorted, neighed, and growled like animals.

Most of this strange behaviour was clearly the work of evil spirits or emerged from people's souls. But many undiscerning leaders claimed it was the Holy Spirit, or that the manifestations were 'prophetic.' Many still do.

But where in the Bible does Jesus behave like this? And where does the Holy Spirit cause people to shout uncontrollably, make animal noises, jump up and down like pogo sticks, shake their heads uncontrollably, or puff like Thomas the Tank Engine?

His fruits are love, joy, peace, forbearance, kindness, goodness, faithfulness, gentleness, and self-control. But these divine qualities are absent in many manifestations that I see.

Any uncontrolled behaviour gives the ground for evil spirits to enter a person. I have seen this happen in many meetings.

International evangelist Torben Sondergaard issued a public statement about them in 2019.

He said: 'In many places, wrong spirits have crept into the church and shown themselves through weird manifestations and shaking.

'Many people today think this is the Holy Spirit manifesting, yet through the years we've prayed for many people who have had these manifestations, and they have experienced a freedom from them through deliverance.

'We've also noticed that many of these wrong spirits, sadly enough, have been received during church meetings.'

History repeats itself

None of this is new. The Welsh revival stopped when its leader, Evan Roberts, withdrew following criticism about manifestations.

He went to live with the Christian Bible teacher, Jesse Penn-Lewis, and her husband.

Mrs Penn-Lewis wrote in her book, War on the Saints: 'As is tragically the case in many powerful works of God, some believers became carried away with emotionalism.

'Others seemed to be influenced by evil supernatural forces that tried to disrupt this genuine outpouring of the Holy Spirit.

'In the face of criticism that he was taking glory for himself, and that the revival was full of emotional excesses, the earnest and devout Roberts withdrew ...'

Tragic.

She continues: 'The aftermath of the revival in Wales, which was a true work of God, revealed numbers of "honest souls" swept off their feet by evil and supernatural powers, which they were not able to discern from the true working of God.

'And later still than the Welsh revival, there have been other "movements," with large numbers of earnest servants of God swept into deception, through the wiles of deceiving spirits counterfeiting the workings of God; all "honest souls," deceived by the subtle foe, and certain to be led on into still deeper deception.

'Not once in the Acts of the Apostles do we find twitching, writhing, convulsions, or other effects of supernatural power on the human frame, recorded as results of being filled with the Holy Spirit.'

I find it amazing that these words, written a hundred years ago, still have such relevance today. And it is tragic that we are unwilling to learn from the past.

Discerning the reactions

Some people's 'Holy Spirit' manifestations are exhibitionism. Others want to show how 'spiritual' they are or impress their leaders or friends. Others manifest demons.

Mrs Penn-Lewis addressed this mixture in War on the Saints.

She wrote: 'From such possessed believers there can proceed, at intervals, streams from the two sources of power; one from the

Spirit of God in the centre, and the other from an evil spirit in the outer man.

'A strange element comes in, possibly only recognisable to some with keen spiritual vision, or else plainly obvious to all.

'Perhaps the speaker begins to pray quietly, and calmly, with a pure spirit, but suddenly the voice is raised, it sounds 'hollow,' or has a metallic tone; the tension of the meeting increases; an overwhelming, overmastering 'power' falls upon it; and no one thinks of 'resisting' what appears to be such a 'manifestation of God!

'The majority of those present may have no idea of the mixture which has crept in.'

Mrs Penn-Lewis goes on to explain that many mature believers put their doubts to one side, because the person had been operating under the power of the Holy Spirit moments earlier.

She adds: 'They can't discern the two separate 'manifestations' coming from the same person.'

Be warned. The Holy Spirit, whose fruit is self-control, will never make you lose control by shouting, laughing, jumping, falling over, or anything else.

Any uncontrolled behaviour is either demonic, or of human origin, or a mixture of the two. So, the input of a seer is so important to discern what is going on.

Paul wrote in 1 Corinthians 14:32: 'The spirits of the prophets are subject to the prophets.' So, no one can say: 'But I just *had* to prophesy, laugh, shout or speak in tongues, I couldn't stop.'

We can all use self-control if we want to.

Jesus' had the Holy Spirit without limit, but there is no record of him twitching, contorting his body, staggering uncontrollably, shouting, or laughing hysterically.

And the New Testament apostles saw more of the Holy Spirit's power than many of us will ever see. But there's no record of them behaving strangely under the power of the Spirit.

Their 'drunken' behaviour at Pentecost was an exception. If it had happened again, it would have been recorded in the book of Acts or in the epistles.

These men saw people healed and delivered, filled with the Spirit, and get saved. But they did not grimace, shout, shake, blow, or contort to get results.

Claiming that the Holy Spirit produces manifestations like these turns the scripture on its head. The *opposite* is true.

In the New Testament, it was *demons* who produced uncontrolled shrieks and shouts. It was the demons who made people shake, vomit, and fall to the ground.

It has been one of Satan's greatest accomplishments to convince thousands of Christians that the Holy Spirit causes this godless behaviour.

We should never assume that a leader or someone with a powerful ministry gets everything right, especially if they are strong characters and are unprepared to test and discuss their activities with you.

That applies to me, you, and every other Christian. We all need seers and Bible teachers to speak without restriction into every area of our lives.

Romans 11:29 says that God's gifts and callings are never withdrawn. This is why it is so importance to get the input of seers and test everything against God's word.

When kingdoms collide

Now, you may occasionally have a dramatic or unusual physical experience when the Holy Spirit fills you. But if you can't pull back from it, then test it.

How? With the truth of the Bible.

The Word of God and the Spirit of God never contradict one another. So, ignore people who justify unbiblical behaviour by claiming that God is doing a 'new thing.'

Ecclesiastes 1:9 says: 'There is nothing new under the sun.' God's 'new things' will always conform to his Word and will never go beyond it.

Having said that, it's not surprising that people physically react when the Holy Spirit touches them. He is the most powerful person on the planet.

It would be strange if we *did not* react when his power collides with our weak humanity.

All hell can break loose. Literally. And heaven. And our emotions. This is completely biblical.

People often shouted, screamed, vomited, or fell under the influence of demons when Jesus and his disciples ministered to them.

In Acts 8:4ff, Philip went to Samaria and ... 'with shrieks, impure spirits came out of many, and many who were paralysed, or lame were healed.'

Shrieks are nothing new. And while they are never from the Holy Spirit, they are not always demonic.

In Matthew 15, a Canaanite woman asked Jesus to help her demon-possessed daughter.

It says she *cried out*, and the Greek words mean she uttered urgent screams or shrieks or used 'inarticulate shouts that express deep emotion'.

Our souls are capable of shrieking or producing other sounds when the Holy Spirit touches a deep wound, a bad conscience, or a trauma.

We need seers and the gift of discernment to work out what is happening.

Where are the watchmen?

Seers have a key role in keeping God's people safe. But few churches have seers, or watchmen and watchwomen to advise the leader and elders.

Habakkuk understood the importance of watching or seeing. Habakkuk 2:1 says: 'I will stand at my watch and station myself on the ramparts; I will look to *see* what he will say to me.'

And Zechariah 13:7 says: 'Strike the shepherd, and the sheep will be scattered.'

So, pastors are vulnerable, and need protection. But not many make space for watchmen, watchwomen and seers, and sometimes label them as negative, divisive or critical.

As a result, church leaders and their congregations become victims of deception, immorality, sickness, divorce, and premature death.

Watchmen and watchwomen aren't always easy to work with, as they tell you things you prefer to not hear.

They go against the flow, and they never shut up ! Isaiah 62:6: says: 'I have posted watchmen on your walls, Jerusalem … they will *never be silent day or night.'*

But their vital role is explained in Ezekiel 3:17: 'Son of man, I have made you a watchman for the people of Israel; so, hear the word I speak and give them warning from me.'

Watchmen will often see evil curses, spells, sins and the devil's plans before the he has a chance to execute them.

They have a vital role in keeping God's people safe, especially when the leader is not a seer.

CHAPTER 12

Other Adventures

Seeing double

The role of the seer can be exciting, as you never know what God will show you next.

I met one man who was carrying two 'anointings'. It emerged that someone else had 'laid a mantle on him' in prayer.

He happily 'took off' those expectations and was free to pursue God's call without conflict.

Another guy seemed to have 'two souls,' and I asked him if he had a twin brother who had died.

He hadn't, but apparently, his mother had lost a son before he was born. This had caused his emotional difficulties as he grew older. But God freed him through prayer.

An apparition in a manse

Norman and Sheila Page were asked to help a family that was being torn apart after moving into an old manse.

The family's little girl never slept well and sometimes saw a female figure dressed in white floating up the stairs without touching the staircase. The apparition left her terrified and in tears.

Norman and Sheila and some friends prayed in the house and cast out the apparition in Jesus' name.

And when they went into the garden, they saw a rubber owl in a tree and sensed a real presence of evil.

They took it down and, on impulse, tore its head off. Inside they discovered newspaper cuttings written in an eastern script. The group sensed that they were curses and broke them in Jesus' name.

When they returned to the house, it felt peaceful and light. The family rows stopped, and the apparition never returned. The little girl slept through the night without fear.

A business transformed

In 2019, I was asked to pray for a businesswoman, whose company was in serious financial difficulty.

When I prayed, I saw several curses that had 'landed' because of some difficulties in the company's past.

I also saw a vision of a framed picture and told the woman: 'You must see the bigger picture, which I believe God has framed for you to look at.' I was puzzled by the wording.

But the woman told me that God had shown her an image of a framed picture nine years earlier, and that she had been falsely accused of mismanagement and fraud.

However, after she broke the curses, work started streaming in.

She secured contracts with two major hotel groups and a large city corporation

Necromancy and death exposed

I once 'saw' a vision of a man lying on a grave, with blue ribbons coming out of it.

I later discovered that this picture illustrated the occult practice of 'grave sucking,' where some proponents say the Holy Spirit appears like a 'sneaky, blue genie-like Aladdin'.

The man was involved in necromancy, a practice forbidden in the Bible. The Holy Spirit is never described as a 'sneaky, blue genie' in scripture. As if! Genies are from the occult.

Another time, I was standing on a beach before visiting a friend who lived nearby, and I saw dead bodies lying around me.

My friend confirmed that people had died in a serious flood many years ago. It explained the sense of death in the village and why churches never flourished.

The hand of God in a car crash

Norman was once driving home exhausted after working long shifts.

He recalls: 'I heard a loud bang, and when I opened my eyes, I realised that I had crashed. I did not feel any impact – the noise woke me up.

'Then I saw an enormous white hand, holding me in my seat.

'It disappeared, and I saw that the airbags were up. I had crossed two lines of rush hour traffic at 50mph and hit the central crash barrier at a 45-degree angle.

'The car was a write-off, with the gears and shafts protruding from the wreckage. But I was unhurt, and my legs were untouched.

'I walked away, unaffected. No flashbacks, no nightmares, no fears or anxieties, and no physical injuries from a crash that probably should have killed me. I was saved by the hand of God.'

CHAPTER 13

How About You?

Raising up seers

I had mixed motives in publishing this book. Part of me wants to look important, and shout: 'Hey, look at me.'

Forgive me, Father. But I also have a passion to see God raise up more seers.

Deep down, I *know* that I have nothing to offer people. I can scarcely tell apples from oranges and depend entirely on God for insight and discernment.

So, he truly takes the glory for every example I have used in this book.

However, I hope I have been able to inspire you to ask him for the gift of discernment and the anointing of the seer.

The church desperately needs both. I don't think it has ever been so blind as it is now.

Jesus warned us about the risk of being deceived in the end times, and it's happening already, possibly in your church.

And these steps will help you get started.

Ask Father God for more of the Holy Spirit

Many Christians believe that the gifts of the Holy Spirit are like pick-and-mix, where you choose what you want and activate them yourself. But this approach is unbiblical.

God is the giver. Jesus said in Luke 11:13: '... how much more will your Father in heaven give the Holy Spirit to those who ask him!'

And 1 Corinthians 21:11 says that the Holy Spirit then distributes the gifts and determines who gets what.

So, don't force his hand by using activation techniques and other unbiblical practices. Gifts are given, not seized, claimed, or activated.

Get hungry

The best way to receive a gift of the Spirit is to show God you're desperate.

1 Corinthians 14:1 says: 'Eagerly desire spiritual gifts, especially prophecy.'

Eagerly means to be deeply committed, to set your heart on something, to burn with a zeal like a boiling kettle ...

If you cultivate a burning desire, Father God will respond. But he remains Lord and has the final say on which gifts you receive and when.

He may use you as a seer, but he may not. If he does, then the anointing will flow naturally. If it doesn't, then accept that God has not given it to you, at least not yet.

If you try to force it, then you risk giving ground to a false spirit.

Stay hungry

There are no short cuts to having insight and discernment. Proverbs 2:3-6 says: 'Cry out to God for discernment and search for it.'

I ask for God's empowerment most days. I need it.

Staying hungry is a lifestyle. The day you think: 'Hey, I can do this now' is the day you stop trusting Father. And possibly the day when he isn't able to trust you for a season.

There are no shortcuts. God doesn't dwell in our 'instant' culture. So, don't be duped in to thinking that God's anointing will come just because someone has prayed for you or laid hands on you.

I remember the great Bible teacher R.T. Kendall asking a congregation of young people: 'Who wants an anointing from God?' Dozens of hands went up.

Then he asked: 'Who wants a life of pain? You won't receive an anointing without it. Stand up now if you want some pain.'

Not many people did.

True anointings come through years of tough discipleship.

Find a mentor

Most ministries are caught, not taught. So, find someone who functions in the gift of discernment and the ministry of the seer and ask them to train you.

Jesus mentored his disciples. Jethro mentored Moses, Elijah mentored Elisha, Eli mentored Samuel, and Paul mentored Timothy.

And persevere. If you don't find someone straight away, ask God, and keep on asking him.

It took me two years to find the right person. And once I found him, I had to change church, abandon my own ministry, and move to a new location. There may be a price to pay. But it will be worth it.

Get your motivation right

Sadly, the 'revelation' gifts sometimes attract the wrong people. So, if you want to 'see' to impress your friends, build a ministry or be the person with God's inside track, then you must repent and ask God to deal with your ambition.

God's gifts and anointings are expressions of his love. Our primary desire must be to see what Father is doing. Then we will see people healed, delivered, or transformed.

Ask for God to open your eyes

God raises up seers. He gives gifts. He imparts anointings. He opens eyes.

Paul wrote in Ephesians 1:17-18: 'I keep asking that the God of our Lord Jesus Christ, the glorious Father, may give you the spirit of wisdom and revelation, so that you may know him better. I pray that the eyes of your heart may be enlightened ...'

This should be our daily prayer.

Don't try and open your own eyes

Many Christians use activation games and techniques to get started in discernment and other gifts of the Holy Spirit.

They have no biblical basis. They can demean the Holy Spirit, and some are based on occult and new age practices.

We should not try to activate the gift of prophecy or any other gift. The Holy Spirit does it. Our role is to lay hands on people. He does the rest.

If you try to activate spiritual gifts yourself, you may end up being influenced by a false spirit.

Only God can initiate true supernatural activity. This is what distinguishes Christianity from new age and the occult practices that require *you* to take the initiative.

Many prophetic activations erroneously put people in the driving seat. Others place you under the spiritual control of a big-name speaker at a conference.

In 1 Kings 18, the prophets of Baal tried all kinds of weird and wonderful methods, including self-harm, to activate fire on Mount Carmel.

But Elijah prayed, and the Lord's fire fell. That's how God's supernatural works. Beware meetings where they try to manufacture God's presence through music, emotionalism, or loud, repetitive drumming.

The term 'activation' belongs to the new age and spiritists. And if you copy occult and new age terminology, you will find it difficult to separate them from the practices they represent.

God forbids all occult practices in Deuteronomy 18: 9-14. And v9 says we should not even *imitate* occult practices. This includes copying their names.

The list in Deuteronomy covers many contemporary practices that masquerade under different names.

Activation games that are rooted in the occult flirt with a demonic spirit of divination which may cause breathing problems.

Satan doesn't play games. Jesus said he comes to kill, steal, and destroy. Be warned.

Be like the people from Berea, described in Acts 17:11. They ... 'received the message with great eagerness and examined the scriptures every day to see if what Paul said was true.'

Dealing with blockages

Some people turn to activations because they cannot receive the fullness of the Holy Spirit.

There are three main reasons why people get stuck, and activations don't resolve any of them.

First, you haven't been given the gift yet.

Second, you don't eagerly desire it.

And third, you have a blockage, such as a curse or you have been involved in the occult.

Jesus said in Mark 16: 17-18 that his disciples would cast out demons and speak in new tongues. So, you might have to deal with demons first.

I speak from experience. After I was saved, I spent months asking God for the baptism of the Holy Spirit.

People prayed for me; I went to Bible weeks, power meetings and I called out to God. But nothing happened.

Then I read that past occult activity can block the Holy Spirit.

So, I renounced my many past sins and destroyed objects, books, and recordings, like people did in Acts 19. And I started speaking in tongues immediately and prophesied the next day.

The same may apply to you. Blockages are common these days, as most people have been involved in the occult, drugs—which is a form of sorcery—new age spirituality, and occult-based apps and games.

All supernatural activity is real. Satan appears as an angel of light.

There are only two sources of supernatural power—God's and the devil's. One is light, the other is darkness. One brings a blessing, the other a curse. They are not two sides of the same coin or like choosing between two flavours of crisps.

If you play the devil's games, there will be a payback. I don't say that to make you afraid, but to keep you from harm.

If you aren't properly delivered from all occult activity or are unclear about the difference between right and wrong, you are unlikely to receive the baptism of the Holy Spirit and will never make progress as a seer.

Surrender your senses to God

Romans 12:1 says: 'Offer your bodies as a living sacrifice, holy and pleasing to God—this is your true and proper worship.'

Our bodies include our senses of sight, hearing, touch, taste, and smell, and we need to offer these to God to use how he wants to. Personally, I do this most days.

Ongoing repentance

God will only let you 'see' into people's lives if you allow him and other people to see into yours.

Matthew 7:5 explains how this works: 'First take the plank out of your own eye, and then you will see clearly to remove the speck from your brother's eye.'

The word *see* in this verse is also used when Jesus healed blind people.

So, if you want to 'see' more, you must walk in transparency and repentance.

This means dealing with your own issues and confessing your sins to God and to trusted friends regularly.

You should never expect to 'see' issues in other people that you have not dealt with in your own life. Matthew 7:5 shows that your own vision will be blocked with a plank.

Seers must live in a permanent attitude of repentance, and continually ask God to examine their hearts.

Create a desire to see things from God's point of view

Seers are as prone to operating in their own strength as any other ministry, and may view things with suspicion, judgement, and pride. If they don't continually deal with this, they risk operating with counterfeit gift of discernment.

God's gifts and anointings are instruments of love. So, true seers will want to help others, to show them mercy and to lead them to the transforming power of Jesus.

They won't just see someone's sin. They will also see their hurting hearts and how the Holy Spirit is seeking to help them.

In Revelation 21:10, John first saw Babylon from the valley, but then saw the new Jerusalem when he was carried to a high mountain.

Seers who just see valleys will never offer hope, only criticism or judgement. We must gaze at Jesus' beauty and fix our eyes on him, as it says in Hebrews 12: 2. There are two aspects to this.

We must look intently at him *and* exclude everything else. I find that the more I do this, the more I see things in other areas.

Are you desperate?

I believe Psalm 62 has the keys for aspiring seers.

Verse 2 reveals our goal: 'So I have looked for You in the sanctuary, to **see** your power and your glory.'

The word *see* is the Hebrew word *chazahi* meaning 'to see as a seer'.

And the preceding verse tells us how to do it: 'You, God, are my God, earnestly I seek you, I thirst for you, my whole being longs for you, in a dry and parched land where there is no water.'

Why not join me in praying that we become so desperate to see God's power and glory that it consumes us and becomes a lifestyle.

It's the only way.

About the Author

Cleland Thom has been bringing insights to God's people for more than 40 years and helps to lead a group called Freedom House.

He was a trustee of a charity that brought God's healing and deliverance to thousands of damaged lives for more than 20 years.

He has spoken and ministered at festivals and conferences, and served on the Evangelical Alliance's Coalition on Occult Issues,

He was leading elder of an Elim church in east London and has appeared on the God Channel, BBC Radio Sussex, Premier Radio, Cross Rhythms Radio and UCB.

He has preached and conducted healing meetings and has trained leaders and leadership teams across the UK. He has also written several books and is a blogger for Cross Rhythms.

He lives in West Sussex and has three sons and four grandchildren.

Printed in Great Britain
by Amazon

62003187R00078